Table of Contents

SHARED RESOURCES

T0059638

MURDER
SPARKS A WAR

Crowds cheered as Archduke Franz Ferdinand and his wife, Sophie, rode in an open car through the streets of Sarajevo, the capital of Bosnia and Herzegovina. The archduke was next in line to become emperor of Austria-Hungary. The empire stretched across Central Europe and into the southern part of the continent, called the Balkans.

Suddenly two shots rang out. The first shot passed through the side of the car, hitting the archduchess. The second shot killed Franz Ferdinand, who died calling for his wife. But Sophie was already dead. It was June 28, 1914, and in a month the world would be at war.

Angry Austrian officials immediately blamed Serbia, a neighbor

A PERSPECTIVES FLIP BOOK

The Split History of

WORLD WAR I

CENTRAL POWERS PERSPECTIVE

BY MICHAEL BURGAN

CONTENT CONSULTANT:
Timothy Solie
Adjunct Professor
Department of History
Minnesota State University, Mankato

COMPASS POINT BOOKS
a capstone imprint

About the Author:

Michael Burgan has written numerous books for children and young adults during his nearly 20 years as a freelance writer. Many of his books have focused on history, geography, and the lives of world leaders. Michael has won several awards for his writing. He lives in Santa Fe, New Mexico, with his cat, Callie.

Source Notes:

Allies Perspective

Page 6, line 5: Hew Strachan. *The First World War*. New York: Viking, 2004, p. 21.

Page 7, line 3: Peter Vansittart. *Voices from the Great War*. New York: Watts, 1984, p. 22.

Page 10, line 2: H.P. Willmott. *World War I*. New York: DK Pub., 2003, p. 56.

Page 10, line 5: Ibid., p. 61.

Page 12, line 6: The August Offensive, the Gallipoli Campaign. New Zealand History Online. 21 May 2013. http://www.nzhistory.net.nz/war/the-gallipoli-campaign/the-august-offensive

Page 12, line 19: Major Thomas S. Bundt, U.S. Army, PhD. "Gas, Mud, and Blood at Ypres: The Painful Lessons of Chemical Warfare." *Military Review*. July–August 2004. The Air University. 21 May 2013. http://www.au.af.mil/au/awc/awcgate/milreview/bundt.pdf

Page 19, line 16: The Lusitania Resource. 21 May 2013. http://www.rmslusitania.info/people/saloon/michael-byrne/

Page 19, line 23: Thomas G. Paterson, et al. *American Foreign Relations: A History*. Vol. 2. Boston: Houghton Mifflin Co., 2005, p. 270.

Page 20, line 12: The National Archives. 21 May 2013. http://www.archives.gov/global-pages/larger-image.html?i=/education/lessons/zimmermann/images/decoded-message-l.jpg&c=/education/lessons/zimmermann/images/decoded-message.caption.html

Page 20, line 16: Wilson's War Message to Congress. World War I Document Archive. 21 May 2013. http://wwi.lib.byu.edu/index.php/Wilson%27s_War_Message_to_Congress

Page 21, line 4: *World War I*, p. 20.

Page 25, line 3: Ibid., p. 220.

Page 25, line 12: "Disclose Pershing's Argument With Foch: Official Document of War Department Tells How American Commander Preserved Identity of A.E. F. as Unit in France." *The Pittsburgh Press*. 9 May 1929. 11 April 2013. http://news.google.com/newspapers?nid=1144&dat=19290509&id=PicbAAAAIBAJ&sjid=BUsEAAAAIBAJ&pg=4317,4124458

Page 26, line 5: James Carl Nelson. *The Remains of Company D: A Story of the Great War*. New York: St. Martin's Press, 2009, p. 283.

Page 27, line 9: President Wilson's Fourteen Points. The Avalon Project: Documents in Law, History and Diplomacy. 21 May 2013. http://avalon.law.yale.edu/20th_century/wilson14.asp

Page 27, line 14: In Their Own Words: Diaries, Memoirs, and Letters of the Past: Diary of George Ludovic Alexander. 21 May 2013. http://www.webmousepublications.com/itow/gla/gla-1118.html

Page 28, line 10: *American Foreign Relations: A History*. Vol. 2, p. 92.

Page 29, line 8: *Voices from the Great War*, p. 263.

Central Powers Perspective:

Page 5, line 13: Autograph Letter of Franz Joseph to the Kaiser. World War I Document Archive. 21 May 2013. http://wwi.lib.byu.edu/index.php/Autograph_Letter_of_Franz_Joseph_to_the_Kaiser

Page 9, line 15: An eye-witness at Louvain. (1914) The History Collection. 21 May 2013. http://digicoll.library.wisc.edu/cgi-bin/History/History-idx?type=turn&entity=History.Louvain.p0005&id=History.Louvain&isize=M

Page 12, line 2: Annika Mombauer. *Helmuth von Moltke and the Origins of the First World War*. Cambridge: Cambridge University Press, 2001, p. 288.

Page 16, line 4: *World War I*, p. 135.

Page 19, line 18: Peter Hart. *The Somme: The Darkest Hour on the Western Front*. New York: Pegasus Books, 2010, p. 93.

Archduke Franz Ferdinand and his wife, Sophie, moments before their deaths

of Bosnia and Herzegovina, for the assassination. Bosnia and
Herzegovina was part of the Austrian empire, but some of its citizens
were Serbs. Serbia had won its independence from the Ottoman
Empire just a few decades before. It then fought two wars to gain
land and influence in the Balkans. Serbia and some Bosnian Serbs
now sought to destroy Austria's rule in Bosnia and Herzegovina.

Serbian leaders denied any role in the killing, although one of
their army colonels had armed the killer, 19-year-old Gavrilo Princip.
Austria's Emperor Franz Joseph, uncle of the dead archduke, also
blamed Russia, which had a formal treaty with Serbia. Russian leader
Tsar Nicholas II and his advisers hoped to weaken Austrian rule in
the region.

Franz Joseph wanted war with Serbia. He said, "The continuance
of this state of things constitutes a constant danger to my house and to
my realm." But going to war with Serbia likely meant taking on Russia
as well. And through treaties, Russia had military ties to France and

Great Britain. Franz Joseph knew his army was too weak to fight so many enemies. He turned to his ally, Germany, for help.

Several German states had been united into one nation less than 50 years before. Germany had become a major power in Europe—feared by the Russians, the French, and the British. Germany had built up its industries and was strengthening its military. Franz Joseph could not win a war unless Germany agreed to help.

Germany's leader, Kaiser Wilhelm II, sent word July 6 that Austria-Hungary could rely on German military aid. With that guarantee, Austria made demands on Serbia. These included cracking down on Serbian groups that opposed Austria. Serbia accepted all but two of the demands—demands that would strip the country of its independence. Austria-Hungary then declared war on Serbia, exactly one month after the assassination.

ONE EMPIRE, MANY GROUPS

The Austro-Hungarian Empire, also called Austria-Hungary, had its roots in lands controlled by the Hapsburgs, a powerful German family. The Austrian branch of the family combined its empire with the kingdom of Hungary in 1867 to create the new, larger empire. Within this vast stretch of Europe were people from many backgrounds. The empire's ethnic groups included Germans, Hungarians, Czechs, Slovaks, Poles, Ukrainians, Serbs, Bosnians, Romanians, Croatians, and Italians. The various religious groups included Protestants, Roman Catholics, Greek Orthodox, Jews, and Muslims. The Hapsburgs let some ethnic groups, such as the Hungarians and Croats, have some political freedoms, but others wanted the same freedoms.

GERMANY AT WAR

Germany declared war on Russia on August 1, and two days later declared war on France, a nation bound by treaty to aid Russia. Meanwhile, the Germans signed a secret treaty with the Ottoman Empire, which included what are now Turkey, Iraq, and Syria. The Ottomans agreed to help Germany in a war against Russia. Germany, the Ottoman Empire, and Austria-Hungary would be known as the Central Powers. The war would pit cousins against each other—Kaiser Wilhelm II and England's King George V were grandsons of England's former queen, Victoria. And Tsar Nicholas II was their cousin.

In Vienna, the capital of Austria, some people celebrated when they heard war was at hand. They were eager to punish Serbia for the assassination of the archduke. Some Germans also welcomed a major European war. They saw it as a way to prove Germany's strength. Kaiser Wilhelm II also believed that France, Russia, and Great Britain, called the Triple Entente, wanted to destroy his country because they feared its growing power. Germany had to fight, and win, to survive.

Within the first week of August, more than 3 million German men began preparing for battle. About 840,000 were in the regular army. Others were called into service, and still others volunteered, eager to show their patriotism and bravery. Many German women also pledged their support, ready to serve as nurses or take jobs formerly held by men. With the people behind the war and the country's military strength, German leaders were sure the Central Powers could win a quick victory.

Germany had expected to fight a war on two fronts—against France in the west and Russia in the east. Its troops began heading in both directions. Forces from Austria-Hungary prepared to enter Serbia. Troops would also head east to fight the Russians. Germany's plan was to keep a small force in the east to fight the Russians while focusing most of its forces on a lightning-fast invasion of France.

To do that German troops would have to first march through Belgium and Luxembourg. On August 2, even before declaring war on France, Germany invaded neutral Luxembourg to seize control of the nation's railways. It would need those tracks to move German troops and supplies into France.

Belgium, like Luxembourg, was a neutral country, and Germany had promised not to invade it. Germany demanded the use of Belgium's railways and for Belgium to allow German troops to enter the country. German leaders warned the Belgians that if their troops resisted, Germany would attack. The Belgians did resist, and soon fighting broke out.

The German army used huge siege guns against the Belgians in 1914.

Germany's invasion of neutral Belgium upset Britain. British leaders had warned the kaiser they would declare war if German forces entered Belgium. With the German invasion, all three nations of the Triple Entente were at war with Germany. Those three nations and the countries that joined them in the war against the Central Powers were called the Allies.

Germany seized control of Belgium's major cities and killed some civilians. By the end of August, most of Belgium was under German control. The British accused Germany of brutality against the Belgians. The Germans said they were just defending themselves against Belgian citizens' attacks. It was later discovered that many of the British accusations were false, reported in the hopes of sparking U.S. support of the Allies. But as the town of Louvain burned, German soldiers fired their guns randomly and taunted the fleeing Belgians. One officer looked at a civilian and said, "The crime is yours"—blaming the Belgians for what was happening.

The Austrians, meanwhile, weren't doing so well with their invasion of Serbia. With some of its troops fighting Russia, the Austro-Hungarian army wasn't strong enough to defeat the Serbs. During an August 17 battle near Serbia's Jadar River, the Austrians suffered 40,000 casualties. The Serbs also captured many of their guns and supplies. Within a few days, the Serbs had forced the Austro-Hungarian army out the country. The Serbs held off another Austrian offensive in December at the Battle of Kolubara. The Central Powers were slowly realizing that this Great War would not end as quickly as they had hoped.

SUCCESSES AND FAILURES

Unlike Austria-Hungary's problems with Serbia, the Germans were having more success on both fronts. In August 1914 the larger German army forced British and French troops to retreat from eastern France during the Battles of the Frontiers. On the Eastern Front the Germans won a huge victory at the Battle of Tannenberg.

The Russians had invaded the East Prussia region of Germany on August 20. The Russians had more soldiers and artillery. But the forests and lakes near the town of Tannenberg gave the Germans defensive barriers and made it hard for the Russians to move troops and supplies. Meanwhile, the Germans had easier access to railways to move men and equipment. By the end of August, the Germans

German sharpshooters prepare for action in 1914.

had trapped thousands of Russians in a forest, while others had retreated. The Germans captured 92,000 Russian troops and killed at least 30,000.

In the west, despite his troops' victories, German general Helmuth von Moltke faced some problems. His forces had advanced quickly. Germany was having trouble keeping them supplied. The German army needed hundreds of tons of food every day, as well as millions of pounds of food for their horses. The troops often relied on captured supplies to survive. The German soldiers were also tiring after weeks of heavy fighting. Still, Germany's plan was to keep heading west and capture Paris, the capital of France.

By this time the French had strengthened their defenses around the Marne River, which cuts across northeastern France. Now they were the ones who could use their own railways to move soldiers and supplies. Meanwhile, the Germans had sent troops back to Belgium.

The Battle of the Marne began September 5, with French and British forces attacking the advancing Germans. The Germans eventually gave up about 45 miles (72 kilometers) of ground they had

The bloody Battle of the Marne claimed hundreds of thousands of casualties.

earlier won. General Moltke saw the Battle of the Marne as a huge defeat. The war so far, he told his wife, with its "rivers of blood," left him "often overcome by dread." Kaiser Wilhelm's son, Crown Prince Wilhelm, told an American reporter, "We have lost the war. It will go on for a long time, but lost it is already." The kaiser, however, said that the Central Powers would still crush their enemies.

In the field German officers had to come up with their next plan. Moltke ordered his men to retreat to the Aisne River in northeastern France. He told them to dig in and prepare to defend their ground. His order led to what became known as trench warfare—both sides positioned in trenches in the ground, with neither side able to force the enemy out.

Despite the defeat at the Marne, Germany still controlled most of Belgium and a part of France that produced important resources, such as coal and iron. The Allies would have to attack well-defended German forces if they wanted to recapture the land they had lost.

SEA AND AIR BATTLES

While the fighting on the Western Front settled into trench warfare, the Great War was extending to the world's seas. Great Britain carried out a naval blockade. Its ships patrolled the North Sea and English Channel. They stopped ships from bringing food and war supplies to the Central Powers.

Great Britain had the world's largest navy. When it came time to challenge the blockade, the Germans turned to a relatively new weapon—the submarine, known in Germany as the U-boat. In February 1915 the Germans declared the waters around Great Britain a war zone. Any ship entering the zone faced a U-boat attack. Germany tested this declaration May 7, when a German submarine fired a torpedo at the British passenger ship *Lusitania* off Ireland's coast. The ship sank, killing nearly 1,200 passengers and crew. Germany said it was justified in its action because the ship was carrying war supplies to Britain.

The Germans also took the war to Great Britain by air. Airplanes were new weapons—the first successful air flight had taken place in 1903. Early in the war, the Germans had sent airships called zeppelins to bomb Allied cities in Europe. The zeppelins were filled with hydrogen, a gas that is lighter than air. Later the Germans developed bomber planes to carry out that mission. The Germans, like the Allies, also used planes over the battlefields. The best-known German pilot was Manfred von Richthofen, who shot down 80 enemy planes. Often flying a red plane, he earned the nickname "the Red Baron." Richthofen was killed in action in April 1918.

A BIGGER WAR

The Central Powers saw both gains and setbacks through 1915. In April at Ypres, Belgium, the Germans used a poisonous gas, chlorine, as a weapon. They used other harmful gases, including mustard gas, later in the war.

German soldiers opened steel tanks to release the chlorine, which drifted over French troops in their trenches. The gas stung the men's eyes and throat, then filled their lungs with pain. The victims coughed and gasped for air as their skin turned a shade of yellowish green. The unlucky ones died as their lungs shut down. The first German gas attacks killed about 5,000 men. The Germans hoped the gas would give them an advantage over the enemy. The French retreated, but gas that remained in the air kept the Germans from advancing. As the fighting continued, the Germans gained some ground, although they could not drive the Allies out of Ypres.

In the Balkans Austria-Hungary hadn't yet defeated Serbia, so Germany sent troops to help do the job. The Turks were facing a major Allied offensive at Gallipoli Peninsula. The British, along with forces from Australia, New Zealand, and France, had landed there in April 1915.

The Central Powers invaded Serbia in October. Bulgaria had now joined the Central Powers, hoping to weaken Russian influence in the Balkans. By the end of 1915, the Central Powers defeated Serbia.

Before this victory the Turks had stopped Allied offensives around Gallipoli, while also fighting the Russians in a region called the Caucasus. And fighting had opened on a new front, between Austria-Hungary and Italy. The Italians had joined the Allies in

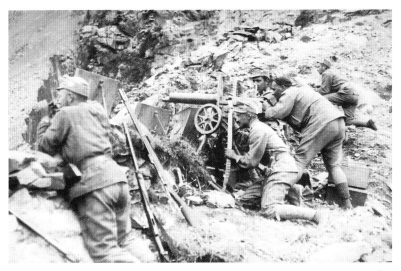

Austrian soldiers aim their machine guns at Italian troops in the Alps.

April 1915. The Austrians and Italians began to fight a series of battles along the mountainous border between Italy and the empire.

Despite their successes, the Central Powers still faced the horrors of trench warfare along the Western Front. German soldiers lived in a series of trenches, often lined with sandbags or wood. Conditions were horrible. Huge rats ran through the trenches, insects swarmed, and the air was often filled with the smell of human waste and dead bodies. By 1916 the Central Powers had built almost 12,000 miles (19,300 km) of trenches on the battlefields of Europe. As the trench warfare went on, the Germans built tunnels to link the trenches, and some men lived as much as 50 feet (15 meters) below ground. Barbed wire guarded the trenches, and attacks usually came at night. Artillery boomed and poison gas filled the air before one side or the other tried to advance. But major victories were hard to win on the Western Front, with both sides so well defended in their trenches. The war dragged on.

THE WAR GETS TOUGH

CH. 3

For weeks the Germans prepared for a major assault on the Western Front. General Erich von Falkenhayn now commanded German forces in the west. He wanted to break the will of French citizens to keep fighting, thinking he could convince them "in a military sense they have nothing more to hope for." He chose the city of Verdun as his target. About 7 a.m. February 21, 1916, German artillery roared into action. Their shells sailed 20 miles (32 km) to strike their targets. The Battle of Verdun had begun.

When the shelling stopped about nine hours later, German infantry poured out of their trenches and began to advance. Some used flamethrowers. Gases forced a stream of oil through a tube

German artillery fires on French forces during the Battle of Verdun.

and the oil was lit just before it sprayed out. The fire usually didn't kill the enemy, but it made them run from their trenches—making them easy targets for German gunners.

At Verdun, after some initial success, the German advance slowed. By March the two sides were fighting a war of attrition. Each side tried to wear down the other and destroy its will to fight. The Battle of Verdun dragged on until December 18—the longest battle of the war. The Germans gained almost no ground and suffered 337,000 casualties, almost as many as the French. The Germans would not launch another major offensive in the west for more than a year.

Austria-Hungary faced difficult times as well. Russia attacked in the east in March, but the Central Powers beat them back. A second offensive came in June. This time the Russians struck at Austrian forces spread out in trenches along the front in Galicia, in what is now Poland and Ukraine. Surprised by the attack, several hundred thousand Austro-Hungarian troops surrendered. The Russians quickly gained ground. Only the arrival of German and Austro-Hungarian reinforcements later in the summer stopped the enemy's advance.

A horse-drawn mobile soup kitchen helped feed the starving Germans.

PROBLEMS AT HOME

The long, painful war was also affecting the civilians of the Central Powers. In Vienna, many public buildings went without heat or light to save fuel for the military. As meat supplies ran low in parts of Austria-Hungary, horses were slaughtered for food.

Germans also faced food shortages. In the capital of Berlin, anger over shortages and high prices led to protests. Often women led these protests, since so many men were off fighting the war. By 1916 the food shortages were leading to health problems for many Berliners. Going into 1917 Germans experienced what they called the "turnip winter." Many people relied on turnips as their main source of food.

Protests were also sparked by politics. Some Germans were socialists who supported the rights of workers and wanted to end the rule of the kaiser. Socialists opposed the war and thought it benefited the rich. On May 1, 1916, German socialists Rosa Luxemburg and Karl Liebknecht led protests against the war in Berlin. Liebknecht was arrested, and the socialists organized strikes. Tens of thousands of Germans refused to work to protest the arrest.

FACING NEW THREATS

The Russians and French made up the largest land forces the Central Powers faced. The British, though, were the driving force behind several new offensives. One was against the Turks, as the British aided Arabs fighting the Ottoman Empire. On the Western Front, the British led an attack against the Germans along the Somme River.

The battle began in late June, as the British bombarded the German trenches with artillery shells. Men watched their friends die and wondered how long the shelling would go on. As a German private named Eversmann recalled, there was the sense of dread about what was to come: "When will they attack—tomorrow or the day after? Who knows?" The British attack on the German lines began July 1. German machine guns mowed down the advancing enemy soldiers, and the British suffered nearly 60,000 casualties in just that day. The fighting would go on for almost five months. In the end, the British and French gained only about 5 miles (8 km) of land. To defend their position, the Germans suffered about 500,000 casualties.

AT SEA AND OVERSEAS

By the end of 1916, Germany had two new military commanders, Field Marshal Paul von Hindenburg and General Erich Ludendorff. Starting in 1917, they began pulling back some of their troops along the Western Front to a new defensive line, the Siegfried Line, known to the world as the Hindenburg Line. The trenches that made up this line ran from the North Sea south to Pont-a-Mousson, France. The new line was easier to defend than the previous ones.

Germany also made a major change in its sea warfare. It had stepped up U-boat attacks through 1916. In January 1917 the German navy announced that its subs would once again attack ships, both enemy and neutral, that entered the waters around Great Britain.

Kaiser Wilhelm II (center) with his commanders, Paul von Hindenburg (left) and Erich Ludendorff

ARMENIAN GENOCIDE

The Ottoman Empire's war against Russia led to
tragedy for the empire's Armenian residents.
Armenians in the Caucasus wanted their own
homeland. The empire's Turkish rulers used the
war as an excuse to kill Armenians or drive
them out of their traditional lands and into
Syria, to the south. Along this forced march,
Turkish troops killed some Armenians. Others
died from starvation, thirst, and disease. As
many as 1.5 million Armenians died because of
Turkish actions. This is known today as the
Armenian genocide—the attempt to wipe out an
entire people.

By this time Germany was seeking new allies, in case the
Americans entered the war. German Foreign Minister Arthur
Zimmermann sent a coded telegram to Heinrich von Eckardt, the
German ambassador to Mexico. In it he said that if the United
States joined the Allies, Germany would help Mexico regain land it
had previously lost to the United States in return for Mexico joining
the Central Powers. U.S. President Woodrow Wilson learned
about this offer. The news, along with Germany's sinking of U.S.
ships, finally brought the United States into the war in April 1917.
Germany would have a new enemy to face in the months ahead.

THE ROAD TO DEFEAT

During 1917 the German military hoped to force Britain's hand with increased U-boat attacks on ships bound for Britain. But the British were prepared to fight on, and they and the French launched another offensive that began in April. Fighting also broke out again around Ypres, Belgium, in July. In both places the Germans were once again able to keep the enemy from capturing much territory, though they paid a high price. In fighting along the Aisne River, the Germans had 168,000 casualties, and at Ypres the number was 260,000.

German storm troopers emerge from a thick cloud of poison gas.

Events in Russia also helped the Central Powers. Earlier in
1917 the Russians had forced their ruler, Nicholas II, from power.
In November socialists called Bolsheviks seized control of the new
government. The new Russian government signed an armistice
to end the fighting between Russia and Germany. A peace treaty
would soon follow. German leaders hoped that the absence of a
major Allied nation would turn the tide of the war in their favor.

With Russia out of the war, Germany could move most of its
eastern troops to the west. Von Hindenburg and Ludendorff then
began to plan a last major offensive against the French and British.
They wanted to strike before the major U.S. force arrived in Europe.

The plan was to defeat the British first, along the northern
sections of the Western Front around the Somme. Ludendorff
counted on small groups of his best soldiers, called storm troopers,

to break through holes in the lines and attack the enemy from behind. He said he was prepared to lose 1 million men in this last great effort to win the war. Ludendorff also realized that new offensives still might not be enough to bring victory. But when peace came, he wanted Germany to control as much land as possible.

WARTIME SUFFERING

As the Germans planned for this assault, the Central Powers entered 1918 as a weak fighting force. Food and natural resources were in short supply. For several years German civilians had been eating ersatz (substitute) food. Coffee was made from barley or dandelion roots. Fake meat was made from flour and mushrooms. In both Germany and Austria, children died in large numbers. More and more German workers went on strike, tired of how they had

Starving Berliners dig through garbage piles looking for food in 1918.

THE HINDENBURG LINE

The Germans began building the Hindenburg Line in 1916. This huge defense system covered nearly 100 miles (160 km) of the Western Front. It was a series of strongholds linked by deep, wide trenches and tunnels and protected by thick belts of barbed wire. Each stronghold held bunkers, which are protected defensive positions, and machine-gun nests made of concrete. As the Germans withdrew to the Hindenburg Line, they flattened everything in front of it so that attackers would have no cover. The Germans believed that the Hindenburg Line was so strong that no army would ever get past it.

suffered during the war. By February Kaiser Wilhelm II realized how his people were hurting. He wanted peace, but he wanted it to come with a German victory. He believed von Hindenburg and Ludendorff's plan would bring that triumph.

The first offensive began in March, near the Somme. The Germans called it Operation Michael, named for Germany's patron saint. The Germans' massive force greatly outnumbered the opposing British troops. The Germans quickly took back some of the ground they had once held. Over the next few months, they launched new attacks and advanced farther into France. But along the way, they suffered high casualties, which included many of the fierce storm troopers. Germany saw what the future held, as more and

An Allied officer leads his soldiers out of the trenches amidst German shelling.

more American troops reached France and entered the battle. By September the Allies had begun to punch through the Hindenburg Line, taking land that Germany had held for four years.

Austria-Hungary was struggling too, as the Italians began a successful offensive. The Ottoman Empire was becoming less willing to help the other Central Powers. It was more concerned with defending its interests than in helping Germany. On the battlefield, some German troops deserted. Ludendorff still dreamed of more military success, but many Germans were tired of war. So were millions of others in Europe and Asia.

REVOLUTION AND PEACE

At the end of September, Bulgaria asked the Allies for an armistice. On October 30 Turkey signed an armistice as well, followed four days later by Austria-Hungary.

As their allies sought to end the war, more Germans spoke out against it. Such talk upset German soldiers along the front, who wanted peace only if it didn't weaken their homeland.

But in the German port of Kiel, sailors refused orders to take their ships to sea. Civilians struggled with continuing food shortages and a new menace—a deadly strain of influenza. The "Spanish flu" struck soldiers too. German socialists stepped up calls for strikes and prepared for a revolution. The government began

A convoy of German soldiers heads to the front in 1918.

to give elected lawmakers more power, but Kaiser Wilhelm II refused to step down. But as protests grew and a revolution broke out, German generals could no longer support the kaiser. It was announced November 9 that Wilhelm was giving up his throne.

Two days later the guns fell silent on the Western Front. Germany had signed an armistice with the Allies. The terms of the agreement said Germany had to give up tens of thousands of weapons and all of its submarines. The Allied blockade would continue. The armistice was just the first step in ending the war. Next would come peace treaties. The Allies wanted a separate one with each defeated Central Power.

In 1919 the Allies met in Paris to write the treaty. The Germans had no say in the details. The final Treaty of Versailles, signed June 28, 1919, angered many Germans. The British and French wanted them to pay a high price for the war. Germany had to accept full responsibility for starting the war and had to pay reparations — money to help the Allies rebuild what the war had destroyed. The treaty also forced Germany to drastically reduce its military and give up its air force. Germany had to give land to France and the newly formed nation of Poland. For Austria-Hungary and the Ottoman Empire, the war meant the end of their empires. Newly independent states were carved out of Austria-Hungary. The Turks gave up large chunks of land to the British and French.

The peace treaty upset Germans for many reasons. They thought it was wrong to blame them alone for starting the war. And they could never pay the reparations the Allies demanded — they were simply too high for a country that had been so weakened by war. Some Germans also believed that their army could have won the war. They said socialists and others who opposed the war had betrayed the German military.

In Germany, anger over the way World War I ended did not fade. A politician named Adolf Hitler was able to use that anger to help win control of Germany. During the 1930s he illegally rebuilt the German military and then launched World War II. A killing in Sarajevo in 1914 started a chain of events that shaped history through most of the 20th century.

A protest led by Adolf Hitler in 1933 against the Treaty of Versailles would eventually lead to another devastating conflict, World War II.

INDEX

SELECT BIBLIOGRAPHY

Chambers, John Whiteclay, II, ed. *The Oxford Companion to American Military History*. New York: Oxford University Press, 1999.

Davis, Belinda J. *Home Fires Burning: Food, Politics, and Everyday Life in World War I Berlin*. Chapel Hill: University of North Carolina Press, 2000.

Fleming, Thomas J. *The Illusion of Victory: America in World War I*. New York: Basic Books, 2004.

Hart, Peter. *The Somme: The Darkest Hour on the Western Front*. New York: Pegasus Books, 2010.

Herwig, Holger H. *The First World War: Germany and Austria–Hungary, 1914–1918*. New York: St. Martin's Press, 1997.

Keegan, John. *The First World War*. New York: A. Knopf, 1999.

Nelson, James Carl. *The Remains of Company D: A Story of the Great War*. New York: St. Martin's Press, 2009.

Paterson, Thomas G., et al. *American Foreign Relations: A History*. Vol. 2. Boston: Houghton Mifflin Co., 2005.

Strachan, Hew. *The First World War*. New York: Viking, 2004.

The Times Documentary History of the War. London: The Times Pub. Co., 1917.

Vansittart, Peter. *Voices from the Great War*. New York: Watts, 1984.

Willmott, H.P. *World War I*. New York: DK Pub., 2003.

FURTHER READING

Barber, Nicola. *World War I*. Chicago.: Heinemann Library, 2012.

Gregory, Josh. *World War I*. New York: Children's Press, 2012.

Heinrichs, Ann. *Voices of World War I: Stories from the Trenches*. Mankato, Minn.: Capstone Press, 2011.

Kent, Zachary. *World War I: From the Lusitania to Versailles*. Berkeley Heights, N.J.: Enslow Publishers, 2011.

Langley, Andrew. *The Hundred Days Offensive: The Allies' Push to Win World War I*. Minneapolis: Compass Point Books, 2009.

Slavicek, Louise Chipley. *The Treaty of Versailles*. New York: Chelsea House Publishers, 2010.

April 25: Allied forces land at Gallipoli Peninsula, Turkey

May 7: A German U-boat sinks the passenger ship *Lusitania*, killing almost 1,200 people

May 23: Italy declares war on Austria-Hungary

1916

February 21: The Germans launch a major offensive around the French city of Verdun

May 31: British and German naval ships fight their last major battle of the war, near Jutland, Denmark

June: The Russians' Brusilov Offensive leads to solid gains in the east, until Central Powers reinforcements stop them

July 1: The main part of the Battle of the Somme begins

May–June: U.S. troops have their first notable successes on the battlefield

September: The Allies break through Germany's last major defensive line; Bulgaria seeks peace with the Allies

November 9: Kaiser Wilhelm II announces he will step down

November 11: The Allies and Central Powers agree to an armistice

1919

January: The Allies begin working on the terms of a peace treaty

June 28: The Treaty of Versailles is signed

TIMELINE

1914

June 28: Archduke Franz Ferdinand of Austria-Hungary is assassinated in Sarajevo, Bosnia and Herzegovina

July 28: Austria-Hungary declares war on Serbia

August 1: Germany declares war on Russia; soon most major European nations join the fighting, with France and Great Britain aiding Russia and Serbia

August: Germany advances through Luxembourg and Belgium into France; Germany defeats Russia at the Battle of Tannenberg

September 5: The Battle of the Marne begins

1915

February: Germany declares the waters around Great Britain a war zone

April: German troops at Ypres, Belgium, use poison gas on the Allies

1917

January: Germany again decides to attack any ships entering British waters

April 6: The U.S. declares war on Germany

June: First U.S. forces reach France

July: The British suffer heavy casualties during the third Battle of Ypres

November: Bolsheviks take control of the Russian government and sign an armistice with Germany in December

1918

January: U.S. President Woodrow Wilson lists 14 Points that he hopes will shape the peace process when the war ends

March: Germany begins the first of a series of offensives along the Western Front

INTERNET SITES

Use FactHound to find Internet sites related to this book. All of the sites on FactHound have been researched by our staff.

Here's all you do:
Visit *www.facthound.com*
Type in this code: 9780756545727

GLOSSARY

ALLIANCE—an agreement between nations or groups of people to work together

ARMISTICE—a formal agreement to end the fighting during a war

ARTILLERY—cannons and other large guns that fire explosives over long distances

ASSASSINATION—the murder of someone who is well known or important

BALKANS—countries on the Balkan Peninsula in southeastern Europe

CASUALTIES—soldiers killed, captured, missing, or injured during a war

ENTENTE—a French word meaning understanding, often used to describe the relationship between nations that agree to help each other

NEUTRAL—not supporting one side or the other in an argument or war

PROPAGANDA—information spread to try to influence the thinking of people; often not completely true or fair

SABOTAGE—damage or destruction that is done on purpose

STRIKE—to refuse to work because of a disagreement with the employer over wages or working conditions

WAR OF ATTRITION—fighting in which each side tries to wear down the other, rather than seeking to gain large areas of land